FOREWORD BY JOSEPH COELHO

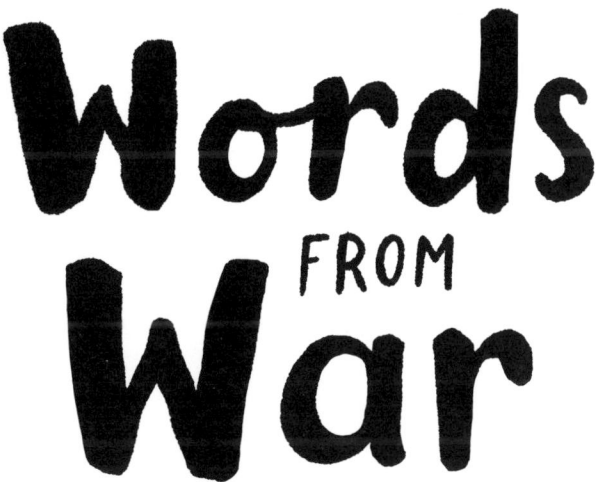

Words from War

A COLLECTION OF POETRY ABOUT CONFLICT

FLORA DELARGY

For Tom. ~ F.D.

HODDER CHILDREN'S BOOKS
First published in Great Britain in 2025 by
Hodder and Stoughton Limited

Foreword text © Joseph Coelho 2025
'Where Does Our Power Lie?' © Joseph Coelho 2025

Full poetry permissions credits on page 78

All other text © Hodder & Stoughton 2025
Illustrations © Flora Delargy 2025

Flora Delargy has asserted their right under the Copyright, Designs
and Patents Act 1988, to be identified as the illustrator of this work.

All rights reserved. A CIP catalogue record for this book is available from the British Library.

HB ISBN: 978-1-444-97388-4
E-book ISBN: 978-1-444-97389-1

10 9 8 7 6 5 4 3 2 1

Printed in China

Hodder Children's Books
An imprint of
Hachette Children's Group
Part of Hodder and Stoughton Limited
Carmelite House, 50 Victoria Embankment
London EC4Y 0DZ

An Hachette UK Company
www.hachette.co.uk
www.hachettechildrens.co.uk

The authorised representative in the EEA is Hachette Ireland,
8 Castlecourt Centre, Dublin 15, D15 XTP3, Ireland (email: info@hbgi.ie)

Every effort has been made to ensure facts about ongoing conflicts were up
to date at the time of going to press. However, events may have unfolded
and circumstances may have changed since the publication of this book.

Words from War

A Collection of Poetry About Conflict

CONTENTS

Foreword by Joseph Coelho 6-8

Extract from the *Iliad* 10-11

Homer 12

The Trojan War 13

'The Charge of the Light Brigade' 14-16

Alfred, Lord Tennyson 17

The Crimean War 18-19

'The Colored Soldiers' 21-23

Paul Laurence Dunbar 24

The American Civil War 26-27

'Dulce et Decorum est' 28-29

'After a Bad Deam' 30

Wilfred Owen 32

Gerrit Engelke 33

The First World War 34-35

'The Butterfly' 36

Pavel Friedmann 37

The Holocaust 38-39

'The War' 40-43

Michael Rosen 44

The Second World War 46-47

'During a War' 48

Naomi Shihab Nye 49

The War on Terror 50-51

Extract from 'The Writer's Rights' 53-54

Asha Lul Mohamud Yusuf 55

The Somali Civil War 56-57

'Lament for Syria' 58-60

Amineh Abou Kerech 62

The Syrian War 64-65

'Letters to a Dead Soldier' 67-68

Maria Docheva 69

The Russia-Ukraine War 70-71

'Where Does Our Power Lie?' 72-74

Joseph Coelho 75

Glossary 76-77

Credits 78-79

FOREWORD

JOSEPH COELHO

Archaeologists have discovered evidence of conflict going back ten thousand years or more. Unfortunately, we are all too aware of how much war continues to be a part of people's daily lives.

Poetry has often been written at times of war, and it is, I believe, the medium best suited to deal with the onslaught of emotions that war brings forth. Poetry is also capable of harshly placing readers squarely in the shoes of another, whether that is the boots of a soldier or the bare feet of a fleeing family. It is because of this that I think poetry has the power to change things, to build our empathy until we all realise the never tired statement that, in war, there are no winners.

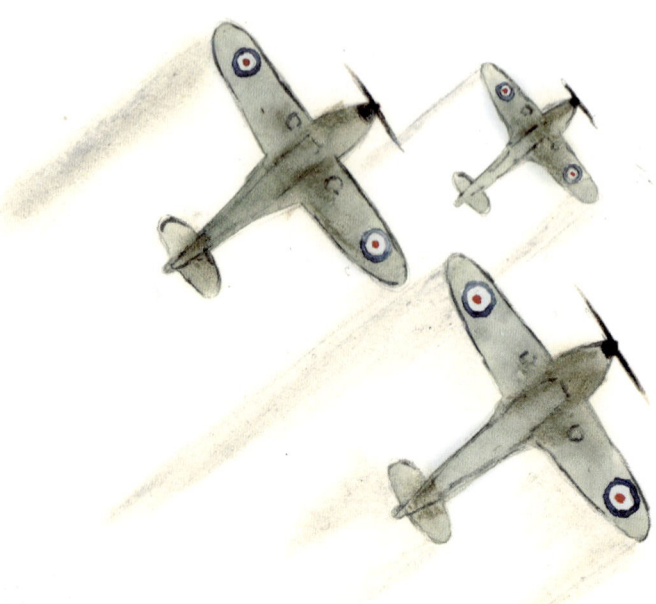

It is my hope that through these poems you will see first hand the impact of wars and their futility both past and present. I hope that these poems will move you to a shared dream of a future where war is never seen as an option because through Homer you will remember the heartache of lost friendships, and through Dunbar the sacrifices made by communities, and through Yusuf the injustices that wars breed, and through Kerech the cultures that wars destroy. Naturally, there are difficult topics covered through these poems – war is, after all, a bloody affair that rips at the heart. But there is also bravery and resilience and inspiration in these verses. There are poems by children who found their voice through poetry, and poems of beauty written in confinement in the darkest of situations. The human spirit never fails to strive forward, never fails to shine, and you will see it at its most vivid within these pages.

So often, talk of war leads to a feeling of hopelessness, but when I talk to young people, I am forever left hopeful. Each generation by definition does things differently, and rails against what has gone before. When I meet with young people, I see bright, wise minds that feel deeply, know their own hearts and care about the hearts of others. That's why I am hopeful that you, dear reader, will help build a future where war is no longer part of the human experience. Where instead, it is poetry that provides our only needed remembrance of what war has previously wrought.

THE ILIAD

HOMER

Extract from **the Iliad, Book 24 – The end of the Trojan War**

The games were over now. The gathered armies scattered,
each man to his fast ship, and fighters turned their minds
to thoughts of food and the sweet, warm grip of sleep.
But Achilles kept on grieving for his friend,
the memory burning on . . .
and all-subduing sleep could not take him,
not now, he turned and twisted, side to side,
he longed for Patroclus' manhood, his gallant heart—
What rough campaigns they'd fought to an end together,
what hardships they had suffered, cleaving their way
through wars of men and pounding waves at sea.
The memories flooded over him, live tears flowing,
and now he'd lie on his side, now flat on his back,

now face down again. At last, he'd leap to his feet,
wander in anguish, aimless along the surf, and dawn on dawn
flaming over the sea and shore would find him pacing.
Then he'd yoke his racing team, to the chariot-harness,
lash the corpse of Hector behind the car for dragging
and haul him three times round the dead Patroclus' tomb,
and then he'd rest again in his tents and leave the body
sprawled face down in the dust. But Apollo pitied Hector—
dead man though he was—and warded all corruption off
from Hector's corpse and round him, head to foot,
the great god wrapped the golden shield of storm,
so his skin would never rip as Achilles dragged him on.

Late eighth or early seventh century BCE

HOMER

Homer was supposedly a blind poet and philosopher, born in ancient Greece sometime between the eighth and ninth century BCE, around 2,800–2,700 years ago. We say 'supposedly', because no one truly knows who Homer was, and there's even a 'Homeric question' as to whether Homer existed at all. Was Homer a group of poets rather than one man? Was Homer a woman?
No one can be certain.

What we do know about Homer is the impact the *Iliad* has had on the world. The *Iliad* is one of the oldest stories still read around the world today and is believed to be the oldest war poem in the world. The *Iliad's* themes of hardships suffered and friends lost resonates with soldiers to this day.

It is very likely that the *Iliad* was originally passed down by people through storytelling, speeches, songs or chants before the story started to be written down. The oldest-known complete version of the *Iliad* is the 'Venetus A' manuscript from the tenth century, which was written a thousand years ago. That's the power of the *Iliad* – people have found so much meaning in it, that it's been passed down, recorded and translated for thousands of years.

THE TROJAN WAR

The Trojan War was a legendary conflict between the early Greeks and the people of Troy (who lived in modern-day Turkey). The war was said to have taken place over 3,000 years ago, so evidence as to whether it really happened is very difficult to find.

According to legend, the war was caused by King Priam of Troy's son, Paris, falling in love with a woman named Helen. Helen was the wife of King Menelaus of Sparta, which was part of Greece. Paris persuaded Helen to flee with him to Troy. The Greeks, wanting Helen back, then launched an attack against Troy.

Troy held out against the attack for ten years. The Greeks eventually won the war through a trick involving the famous Trojan horse. The Greeks built a huge, hollow wooden horse that many warriors hid inside. The rest of the Greek army then pretended to abandon the fight, leaving the horse behind. The Trojans took the horse inside the walls of Troy as an offering to Athena, goddess of wisdom. But during the night, the warriors hiding inside the horse came out and opened the city's gates, allowing the Greeks to come in and destroy Troy.

The story of the Trojan War fascinated the ancient Greeks and features in many works of literature, including the *Iliad*. The extract in this book is taken from the opening of the *Iliad's* final book, Book 24, when the war is over. The Greek hero Achilles is mourning his best friend, Patroclus, who was killed in the war by the Trojan prince Hector. Achilles wants to parade Hector's dead body around as revenge for his loss, but Hector's body is protected by Apollo, the god of sun, light and healing. Achilles is forced to face his grief instead. Achilles' love for his lost friend and his desire for vengeance is a pain felt by many soldiers.

While scholars are on the fence as to whether the Trojan war is fact or fiction, the behaviour of the soldiers in the *Iliad* is all too human and real.

THE CHARGE OF THE LIGHT BRIGADE

ALFRED, LORD TENNYSON

Half a league, half a league,
Half a league onward,
All in the valley of Death
   Rode the six hundred.
"Forward, the Light Brigade!
Charge for the guns!" he said.
Into the valley of Death
   Rode the six hundred.

"Forward, the Light Brigade!"
Was there a man dismayed?
Not though the soldier knew
   Someone had blundered.

Theirs not to make reply,
Theirs not to reason why,
Theirs but to do and die.
Into the valley of Death
Rode the six hundred.

Cannon to right of them,
Cannon to left of them,
Cannon in front of them
　Volleyed and thundered;
Stormed at with shot and shell,
Boldly they rode and well,
Into the jaws of Death,
Into the mouth of hell
　Rode the six hundred.

Flashed all their sabres bare,
Flashed as they turned in air
Sabring the gunners there,
Charging an army, while
　All the world wondered.
Plunged in the battery-smoke
Right through the line they broke;
Cossack and Russian
Reeled from the sabre stroke
　Shattered and sundered.
Then they rode back, but not
　Not the six hundred.

Cannon to right of them,
Cannon to left of them,
Cannon behind them
　Volleyed and thundered;
Stormed at with shot and shell,

While horse and hero fell.
They that had fought so well
Came through the jaws of Death,
Back from the mouth of hell,
All that was left of them,
  Left of six hundred.

When can their glory fade?
O the wild charge they made!
  All the world wondered.
Honour the charge they made!
Honour the Light Brigade,
  Noble six hundred!

1854

ALFRED, LORD TENNYSON
1809-1892

Alfred, Lord Tennyson was an English poet, and the Poet Laureate from 1850–1892.

Tennyson was the fourth son of twelve children. He attended the prestigious Trinity College, Cambridge, but left without completing a degree when money grew tight after the death of his father. Despite this, Tennyson went on to publish several volumes of poetry and become one of the most well-known Victorian writers.

As Tennyson was Poet Laureate during the Crimean War, it was his job to mark or celebrate major national events by writing a new poem. 'The Charge of the Light Brigade' was published on 9 December 1854 in *The Examiner* newspaper, so will have first been read by the public over a month after the charge itself, which happened on 25 October 1854 – that length of delay in reporting a news story was common in Victorian times. Tennyson's poem would have brought the fight to the attention of the British public and is a moving tribute to courage and heroism in the face of devastating defeat, as well as a report of the fatal mistake that sent hundreds of soldiers into a terrible assault.

Tennyson died on 6 October 1892 at his home in Surrey, UK. He was aged 83.

THE CRIMEAN WAR

The Crimean War (1853–1856) broke out between Russia and an alliance of Turkey, Britain, France and Sardinia. It was fought on the Crimean Peninsula in modern-day Ukraine, and claimed an estimated 650,000 lives.

Russia's ruler, Tzar Nicholas I, was attempting to expand his influence over the Middle East and eastern Mediterranean at the expense of the declining Ottoman (Turkish) Empire. The British and French, in turn, saw Tsar Nicholas' power grab as a danger to their trade routes and were determined to stop him. The start of the war was further sparked by religious tension between Catholics and Orthodox Christians. Many Russians were Orthodox, and there were disagreements over access to Jerusalem and other places under Turkish rule that were considered sacred by both Christian sects.

The Crimean War was managed and commanded poorly on both sides. Thousands of casualties suffered from diseases such as cholera and typhoid, which broke out in the soldiers' dirty hospital conditions – and it was during this war that nurses Mary Seacole and Florence Nightingale made huge advances in medicine, statistics and the treatment of sick and wounded soldiers.

From the beginning, the war was plagued by a series of misunderstandings and tactical errors, including the event recounted in 'The Charge of the Light Brigade'.

In 1854, due to a mistake possibly made from a misheard order, some 670 British soldiers were sent to charge in the wrong direction into a terrible assault of 25,000 Russian soldiers. This charge doomed the Light Brigade, and many died or received terrible injuries in the battle.

News of this catastrophe quickly reached Britain. The Crimean War was the first campaign to be reported on by a war correspondent, William Howard Russell of *The Times*. The news led to serious questioning and anger towards the commanders, contrasting with an appreciation of the bravery and sacrifice of the ordinary soldiers, a mood captured by Tennyson in his poem.

The Crimean War ended in 1856 when the Russians surrendered in the face of overwhelming opposition force, signing the Treaty of Paris in March 1856.

THE COLORED SOLDIERS

PAUL LAURENCE DUNBAR

If the muse were mine to tempt it
And my feeble voice were strong,
If my tongue were trained to measures,
   I would sing a stirring song.
I would sing a song heroic
   Of those noble sons of Ham,
Of the gallant colored soldiers
   Who fought for Uncle Sam!

In the early days you scorned them,
   And with many a flip and flout
Said "These battles are the white man's,
   And the whites will fight them out."
Up the hills you fought and faltered,
   In the vales you strove and bled,
While your ears still heard the thunder
   Of the foes' advancing tread.

Then distress fell on the nation,
   And the flag was drooping low;
Should the dust pollute your banner?
   No! the nation shouted, No!
So when War, in savage triumph,
   Spread abroad his funeral pall—
Then you called the colored soldiers,
   And they answered to your call.

And like hounds unleashed and eager
    For the lifeblood of the prey,
Spring they forth and bore them bravely
    In the thickest of the fray.
And where'er the fight was hottest,
    Where the bullets fastest fell,
There they pressed unblanched and fearless
    At the very mouth of hell.

Ah, they rallied to the standard
    To uphold it by their might;
None were stronger in the labors,
    None were braver in the fight.
From the blazing breach of Wagner
    To the plains of Olustee,
They were foremost in the fight
    Of the battles of the free.

And at Pillow! God have mercy
    On the deeds committed there,
And the souls of those poor victims
    Sent to Thee without a prayer.
Let the fulness of Thy pity
    O'er the hot wrought spirits sway
Of the gallant colored soldiers
    Who fell fighting on that day!

Yes, the Blacks enjoy their freedom,
    And they won it dearly, too;
For the lifeblood of their thousands
    Did the southern fields bedew.
In the darkness of their bondage,
    In the depths of slavery's night,
Their muskets flashed the dawning,

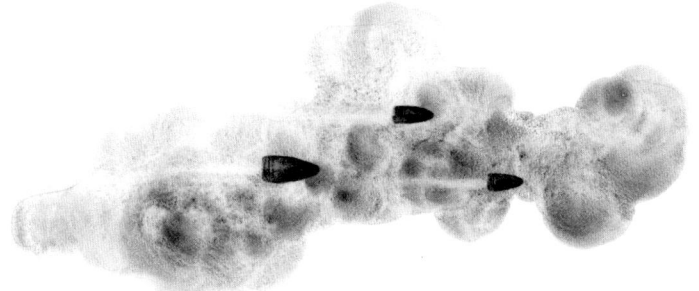

And they fought their way to light.

They were comrades then and brothers.
   Are they more or less to-day?
They were good to stop a bullet
   And to front the fearful fray.
They were citizens and soldiers,
   When rebellion raised its head;
And the traits that made them worthy,—
   Ah! those virtues are not dead.

They have shared your nightly vigils,
   They have shared your daily toil;
And their blood with yours commingling
   Has enriched the Southern soil.

They have slept and marched and suffered
   'Neath the same dark skies as you,
They have met as fierce a foeman,
   And have been as brave and true.

And their deeds shall find a record
   In the registry of Fame;
For their blood has cleansed completely
   Every blot of Slavery's shame.
So all honor and all glory
   To those noble sons of Ham—
The gallant colored soldiers
   Who fought for Uncle Sam!

1901

PAUL LAURENCE DUNBAR
1872-1906

Paul Laurence Dunbar was an African American poet and novelist. He was one of the first black poets to be celebrated in American literature.

Dunbar loved writing and became well known for his words while still in high school in Dayton, Ohio. The only African American in his class, he became president of the school literary society, editor-in-chief of the school paper and class poet.

Dunbar's parents had been enslaved in Kentucky. Joshua Dunbar had escaped from a life of slavery and fought with a Massachusetts regiment in the War Between the States.

Dunbar died on 9 February 1906 aged just 33, after years of health problems and suffering from tuberculosis. He wrote and published until his death.

THE AMERICAN CIVIL WAR

The American Civil War (1861–1865) was the United States of America's most divisive conflict, pitting the Union Army against the Confederate States. With some 620,000 soldiers killed and millions more injured, it was also America's deadliest.

There were several causes for the American Civil War, and tensions came to a head when Abraham Lincoln, a Northern politician (but born in Kentucky and raised in Indiana) who planned to outlaw slavery, was elected president. The Southern economy's backbone was plantation agriculture (large farms), and enslaved black people were forced to do the gruelling work on the plantations for free, so abolishing slavery would harm the South financially. As a result of this, eleven Southern states seceded (formally withdrew) from the United States Union and formed the Confederate States of America. The Union States feared the secession would break up the other remaining states, and so war was declared, with more than 50 major battles being fought over several years.

While the Civil War was first and foremost an economic power struggle between Northern and Southern politicians and businessmen, many Americans were against slavery, and America was the largest slaveholding country in the world. Enslaved black people were horribly mistreated, lived in appalling conditions, and were prohibited from learning to read and write, as well as having all rights stripped from them, such as the right to buy and own property.

President Lincoln issued the Emancipation Proclamation in 1863, which declared that all enslaved people would be freed. This meant that the Confederate States lost a lot of the people doing their work, and provided moral inspiration for the North. It also allowed the recruitment of black soldiers, like Paul Laurence Dunbar's father Joshua, into the Union Army. It was the black soldiers who fought bravely for their right to freedom – some 186,000 of them – that are celebrated in 'The Colored Soldiers'.

The war ended in Confederate surrender in 1865. Although it took years for the practice to really end, slavery was officially abolished in the entire country.

DULCE ET DECORUM EST

WILFRED OWEN

Bent double, like old beggars under sacks,
Knock-kneed, coughing like hags, we cursed through sludge,
Till on the haunting flares we turned our backs,
And towards our distant rest began to trudge.
Men marched asleep. Many had lost their boots,
But limped on, blood-shod. All went lame; all blind;
Drunk with fatigue; deaf even to the hoots
Of gas-shells dropping softly behind.

Gas! GAS! Quick, boys!—An ecstasy of fumbling
Fitting the clumsy helmets just in time,
But someone still was yelling out and stumbling
And flound'ring like a man in fire or lime.—
Dim through the misty panes and thick green light,
As under a green sea, I saw him drowning.

In all my dreams before my helpless sight,
He plunges at me, guttering, choking, drowning.

If in some smothering dreams, you too could pace
Behind the wagon that we flung him in,

And watch the white eyes writhing in his face,
His hanging face, like a devil's sick of sin;
If you could hear, at every jolt, the blood
Come gargling from the froth-corrupted lungs,
Obscene as cancer, bitter as the cud
Of vile, incurable sores on innocent tongues,—
My friend, you would not tell with such high zest
To children ardent for some desperate glory,
The old Lie: *Dulce et decorum est*
Pro patria mori.

Latin phrase is from the Roman poet Horace:
"It is sweet and fitting to die for one's country."

1917

AFTER A BAD DREAM

GERRIT ENGELKE

After a Bad Dream
I am a soldier in the field,
Aware of no-one in the world.
I can't enjoy this rainy day,
So sad and tender, damp and grey,
Because, last night, your face destroyed
My sleep, and brought me to your side.

I am a soldier in the field,
Armed, and a long way from the world.
I'd bar the door, were I at home,
And be alone, where none could come:
Into the deep snug cushions sinking,
I'd close my eyes, and see you in my thinking.

I am a soldier in the field
Of grief, outside the human world.
Rain sings, and streaming waters run,
And I can only fire my gun.
I do it. Must I do it? I know not.
Into the fog, a ringing rifle-shot!

1918

Translated from German by Timothy Adès

WILFRED OWEN
1893-1918

Wilfred Owen was a British poet and soldier.

Owen arrived at the Western Front in France in January 1917, and he soon experienced the violence of war. On one occasion, he was knocked unconscious when he fell into a shell hole, and on another he was blown into the air by a trench mortar.

In June 1917, Owen was sent to Craiglockhart War Hospital, where he spent four months recovering from 'shell shock', which is recognised today as Post Traumatic Stress Disorder, an anxiety disorder caused by the sufferer experiencing very stressful or frightening events. It was at Craiglockhart that Owen met fellow war poet and likely romantic partner Siegfried Sassoon, who influenced his poetry to speak out against the British government's attitude of war being a heroic adventure, and include the shocking realism drawn from his experiences on the front. Though Owen could have taken offers to sit out the rest of the war, he returned to the front to help the men he felt he had left behind. On 4 November 1918, a week before the war's end, Owen was seen leading and encouraging his men, but he was killed in combat, aged 25. After his death, he was awarded the Military Cross for his bravery.

The telegram notifying Owen's family of his death arrived midday on 11 November, just an hour after the celebratory bells of the Armistice rang out.

GERRIT ENGELKE
1890-1918

Gerrit Engelke was a German poet and soldier.

When the First World War broke out, Engelke joined the German Army. From February 1915, he fought at several battles on the Western Front, the area of Europe where most of the trench warfare took place, and was awarded a military medal. In 1917, he was wounded and sent home to recover. During this period, he met his fiancée, Annie-Mai, who is likely the person being addressed in 'After a Bad Dream'.

During the war, several of Engelke's friends were killed. He initially struggled to write poetry about the trauma he was experiencing, but eventually wrote several poems about the war.

On 11 October 1918, only a few weeks before the war was declared over, Engelke was badly wounded and taken prisoner. He died two days later in a British field hospital in France, aged 28.

THE FIRST WORLD WAR

The First World War (1914-1918) saw the Central Powers – consisting of Germany, Austria-Hungary and Turkey – pitted against the Allies – Britain and Ireland, France, Belgium, Russia and later the United States of America. However, the conflict became known as The Great War, because it affected people all over the world.

Many of the First World War's battles were fought using trench warfare. Trenches were long, narrow ditches dug in the ground that soldiers lived in. In between the Allied and German trenches was 'No Man's Land', which soldiers crossed to attack the other side. Entering No Man's Land was very dangerous because there was little or no shelter and protection.

One means of attacking the enemy was by using poison gas, as described by Owen in 'Dulce et Decorum est'. Poisonous chlorine caused coughing, choking, vomiting and even death. The fear and threat of gas were just as powerful as the gas itself, as it terrified soldiers.

In addition to the constant threat of attack, conditions in the trenches were terrible. Many soldiers like Wilfred Owen suffered from 'shell shock', or Post Traumatic Stress Disorder, a condition commonly experienced by soldiers today. Someone with PTSD typically relives traumatic events they've experienced through nightmares and flashbacks, and may feel loneliness, anger and guilt.

The poetry of the First World War changed how people felt about war. Countries' governments had presented war as an adventure to encourage people to enlist, and to die for one's country was considered a heroic, noble thing to do. Owen's poem even concludes with a Latin phrase meaning 'it is sweet and fitting to die for one's country'. But he also says this was 'the old Lie' – that there is no glory in such terrible pain and sacrifice. As the grim reality of war set in, soldiers began to question whether what they were doing was right or necessary, such as Engelke writing 'I can only fire my gun . . . Must I do it?' Many soldiers did not believe in – or even know – the cause they were fighting for.

The war finally ended at 11 a.m. on 11 November 1918.

THE BUTTERFLY

PAVEL FRIEDMANN

The last, the very last,
So richly, brightly, dazzlingly yellow.
Perhaps if the sun's tears would sing
      against a white stone. . . .

Such, such a yellow
Is carried lightly 'way up high.
It went away I'm sure because it wished to
      kiss the world good-bye.

For seven weeks I've lived in here,
Penned up inside this ghetto.
But I have found what I love here.
The dandelions call to me
And the white chestnut branches in the court.
Only I never saw another butterfly.

That butterfly was the last one.
Butterflies don't live here,
      in the ghetto.

1942

Translated from German by Hana Volavkova

PAVEL FRIEDMANN
1921-1944

Pavel Friedmann was a Jewish poet from Czechoslovakia (today split into the Czech Republic and Slovakia). He became famous for his poem 'The Butterfly' after he died.

Friedmann was born in Prague, Czech Republic, and little is known about his early life, perhaps because Nazis often destroyed the records of the Jewish people they kidnapped. He wrote 'The Butterfly' in 1942 when he was being held in Theresienstadt concentration camp. The poem, along with several of his other poems, were discovered after the liberation of Czechoslovakia from Nazi occupation, and then donated to the National Jewish Museum in Prague.

On 29 September 1944, Friedmann was deported to Auschwitz concentration camp, where he was murdered. He was 23.

THE HOLOCAUST

The Holocaust (1941-1945) was a period during the Second World War when people were killed on a scale never seen before, including six million Jews. They were murdered just because of who they were.

The killings were organised by Germany's Nazi party, led by Adolf Hitler. Many German people were poor and hungry following the First World War, as Germany had to pay a lot of money to the countries that won. The Nazis promised hopeful change and a restoration of greatness to the German people, so they rose in popularity and were elected into power in 1933.

From the moment the Nazis formed the government, they persecuted people who they disliked. Nazi ideology was racist, nationalist and anti-democratic. The party seized control using violence and intimidation, and it abolished all other political parties so that no one could stand against them. Jews were forced to live in ghettos like the one Pavel Friedmann wrote 'The Butterfly' in, where they were controlled and often forced into poverty. They were also made to wear a yellow star, to ensure everyone knew they were Jewish.

The Nazis targeted other groups of people, too, including Roma, black and disabled people. They also arrested and took away the rights of other groups, like gay people and political opponents.

The Nazis set up concentration camps where they sent people they disliked. Some were labour camps, some were transit camps to process prisoners, and six were death camps, where the Nazis would kill people, including Pavel Friedmann, in horrendously large numbers. Many people were murdered by camp guards for no reason, and many more died of starvation and sickness.

The Second World War broke out when Nazi Germany invaded other countries. Britain, the US, the Soviet Union and their allies fought back, and as soldiers fighting Germany made their way across areas of Europe controlled by the Nazis, they began to discover the concentration camps. The Nazis, seeing they were going to lose the war, tried to hide the evidence of their crimes by destroying the camps.

But the Nazis were not able to hide what they had done. Today, the enormity of the Holocaust as the worst genocide in history is recognised across the world. It is important to remember it, and what led to it, to try and stop anything like it from happening again.

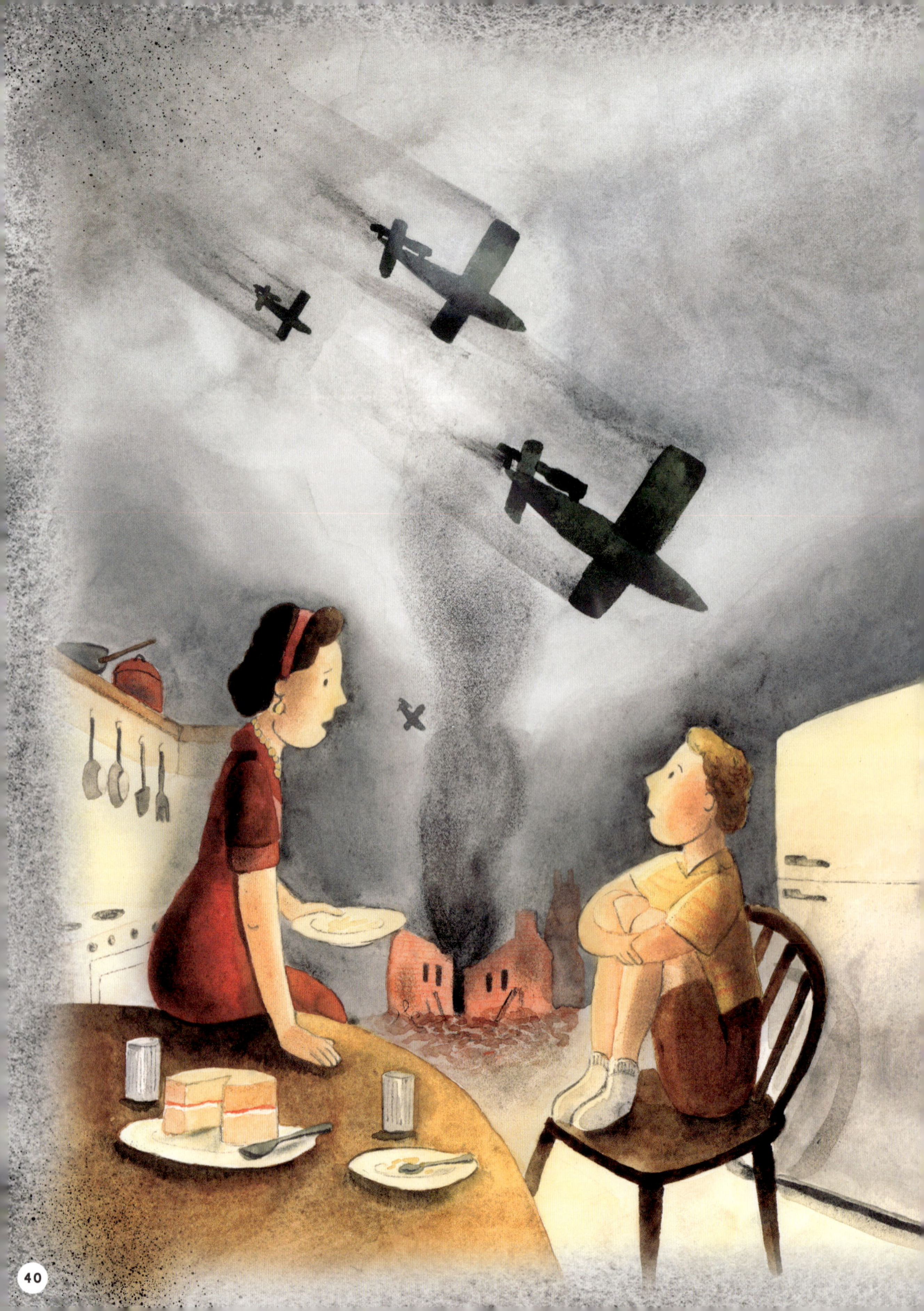

THE WAR

MICHAEL ROSEN

In the evening, after we've eaten,
Mum tells about the War.

"Doodlebugs," she says,
"were bombs that came
flying over us –
rockets, they were,
and they made a noise,
but when the noise stopped
you knew that it was about to drop.
They said you had to run for cover.
If you were out, they said,
the best place to go was in the gutter,
lie down in the gutter.
Once, when I had just come out
of White City Station,
I heard one.
The noise stopped.
They said you had ten seconds to hide
so I ran towards the gutter,
counting to ten,

and I lay down in the gutter and waited.
It landed just up the road from me."

"You lay down in the gutter, Mum? Really?"

In the evening, after we've eaten,
Mum tells about the War.

She says that they thought it wouldn't be long
before Hitler would land in Britain
but then she tells us about what happened in Russia.
She says the Siege of Leningrad was so bad
and that people got so hungry they ate rats.
She says that people crowded round the radio
because they knew that if Hitler won in Russia
nothing would stop him.
"If he had come here," she said,
"we wouldn't be alive.
You wouldn't have been born," she said to me.

We listened to the reports of the
Battle of Stalingrad.
"You see," she said,
"Hitler's troops were lined up here . . ."
And she started moving the plates
and jugs and sauce bottle round the table.
"The Russians were here.
There was a moment when we thought
it was all over and the Russians had lost
and it would be all over for us.
But then, look – "
she moved the jugs and plates again –
"they won!
We couldn't believe it."

She stops.
She stares.
They lost millions.
Millions and millions of people died.

In the evening, after we've eaten,
Mum tells about the war.

2020

MICHAEL ROSEN
1946-

Michael Rosen is a British author and poet. He has written and collaborated on over 150 books of stories, jokes and poetry for all ages, though he is especially well known for his books for children. He is a Professor of Children's Literature at Goldsmiths, University of London, and has received awards both for his writing and his work in education.

Rosen grew up as part of a Jewish-Polish family in London. He noticed that people seemed to be missing from his family history – that there were aunts and uncles who had been there before the Second World War, but who weren't there after. His determination to find out what happened to his relatives lost during the Holocaust and to remember them, as well as record his own memories of the war, has inspired his poetry for years.

A former Children's Laureate, Rosen remains one of the most familiar voices in British children's literature today.

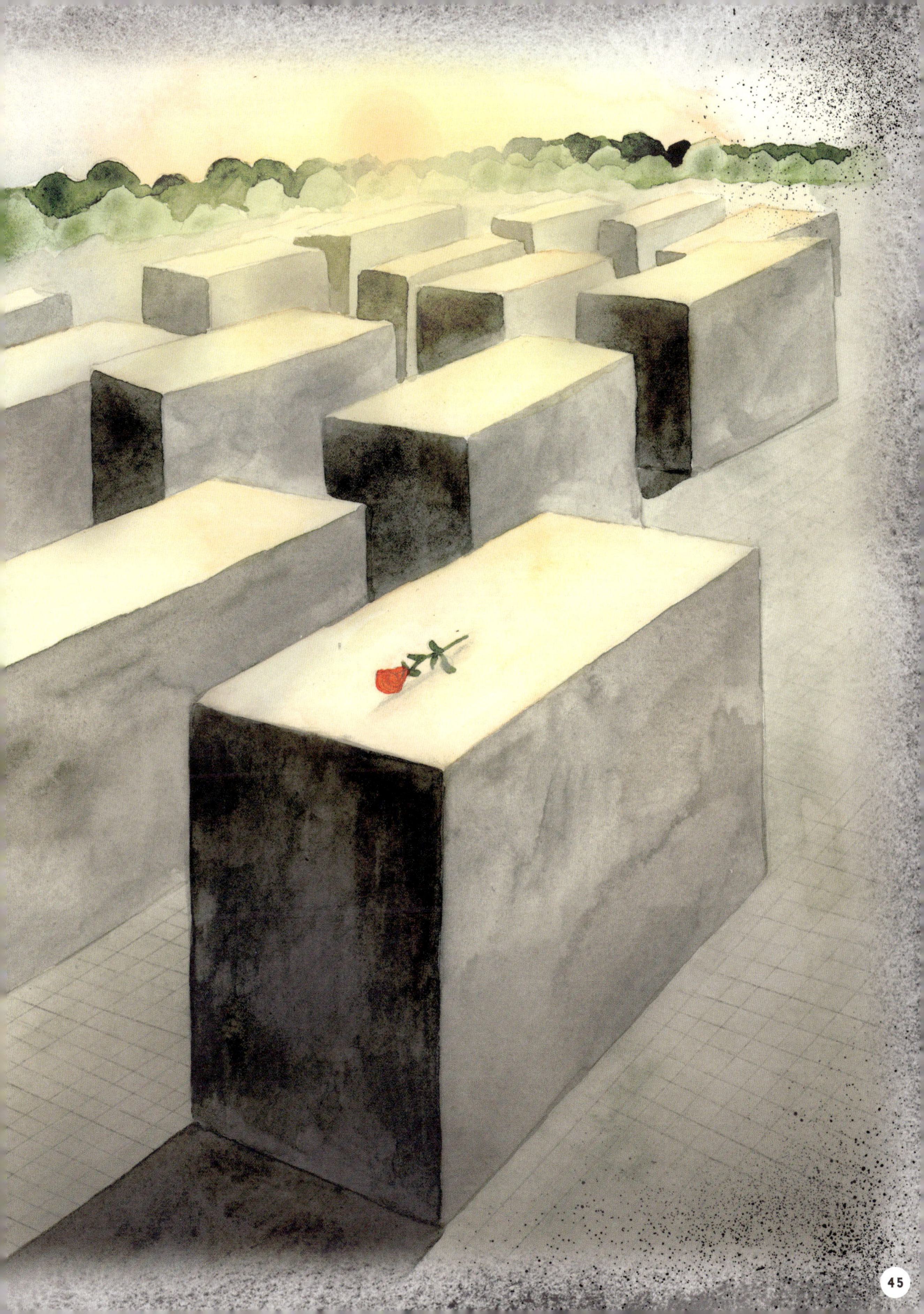

THE SECOND WORLD WAR

The Second World War (1939–1945) had many causes, such as Adolf Hitler (who had plans to invade and take over other countries) becoming Chancellor of Germany in 1933. War was declared when Germany invaded Poland in 1939. The war saw the Axis Powers of Germany, Italy and Japan pitted against the Allies – Britain, France, China, the Soviet Union (now Russia) and the United States of America. However, similarly to the First World War, people all over the world were affected.

The Second World War was the largest conflict in human history. Michael Rosen's poem 'The War' references specific events of the Second World War as remembered by his mother, who was living in London during the Blitz. The Blitz was a German bombing campaign against the United Kingdom, in 1940 and 1941. Bombs like doodlebugs were dropped on large cities in the UK. The bombs caused over 30,000 civilian casualties and left hundreds of thousands homeless. Since these air strikes could happen at any time, people had to find shelter where they could – from underground rail networks to gutters.

Rosen also writes about the war in the Soviet Union, like the prolonged siege of the city of Leningrad (today called St. Petersburg) by German and Finnish armed forces. It lasted from 8 September 1941 to 27 January 1944 – 872 days – but is often called the 900-day siege. Leningrad was almost completely encircled, with all its supply lines cut off. The people inside Leningrad were trapped and left to endure extreme famine, starvation, disease and shelling from long-distance German weapons. About 650,000 Leningrad lives were claimed in 1942 alone. The siege was ended by a successful Soviet offensive driving the German forces, away from the city's outskirts.

The Battle of Stalingrad from July 1942 to February 1943, also noted in Rosen's poem, was one of the deadliest battles of the Second World War. Though Russia successfully defended Stalingrad (now Volgograd) against German advances, it came at a cost: over 800,000 Soviet soldiers were killed. Meanwhile, Soviet forces are estimated to have lost over 1 million soldiers, and around 40,000 civilians died after terrible suffering. The siege of Leningrad and the Battle of Stalingrad are just two of hundreds of battles that took place over the six years of war.

Because the scale of the Second World War was so huge, with many battles of note taking place all over the world, there was not one event or moment that marked its end, but rather several. Hitler's suicide in April 1945 leading to Germany's surrender a month later, and Japan's surrender in September 1945 following the American atomic bombings of Hiroshima and Nagasaki, were both major milestones. The estimated 40–50 million deaths during the Second World War make it the deadliest conflict in history.

DURING A WAR

NAOMI SHIHAB NYE

Best wishes to you & yours,
he closes the letter.

For a moment I can't
fold it up again –
where does "yours" end?
Dark eyes pleading
what could we have done
differently?
Your family,
your community,
circle of earth, we did not want,
we tried to stop,
we were not heard
by dark eyes who are dying
now. How easily they
would have welcomed us in
for coffee, serving it
in a simple room
with a radiant rug.
Your friends & mine.

2005

NAOMI SHIHAB NYE

1952-

Naomi Shihab Nye is an award-winning Palestinian-American poet, editor, author and songwriter. She began writing poetry at the age of six.

Nye was born in St. Louis, Missouri, USA. Her mother was an American of German and Swiss descent, and her father, Aziz Shihab, was a Palestinian journalist. He and his family became refugees in the 1948 Nakba when the state of Israel was created.

Nye spent her childhood in Ramallah in Palestine, the Old City in Jerusalem, and San Antonio, Texas, USA, and she continues to live and work in San Antonio. Nye is a professor of creative writing at Texas State University, and she often teaches writing workshops, mostly to children.

The War on Terror

The War on Terror describes the US-led global counterterrorism campaign launched in response to the terrorist attacks of 11 September 2001, commonly known as 9/11.

On 9/11, four coordinated terrorist attacks were carried out by the group al-Qaeda against the United States of America, in which 19 terrorists hijacked (took control of) four passenger planes. The hijackers crashed the first two planes into the Twin Towers of the World Trade Center in New York City. The third plane struck the Pentagon, the headquarters of the US Department of Defense in Arlington County, Virginia, while the fourth plane crashed in rural Pennsylvania – unplanned – because the passengers aboard that flight managed to fight back against the hijackers. The 9/11 attacks killed 2,977 people and injured more than 6,000 others, making it the deadliest terrorist attack in world history.

In response to the attacks, the United States waged war to eliminate groups like al-Qaeda, deemed terrorist organisations, as well as the foreign governments appearing to support them in Afghanistan, Iraq, Syria and several other countries. The first years of the war saw hundreds of terrorist suspects around the world arrested. The capture and elimination of many of al-Qaeda's senior members, and the overthrowing of dictator Saddam Hussein in Iraq in 2003, were considered further victories by the US government.

However, the war in Afghanistan caused the al-Qaeda network to scatter, making its members even harder to find. Bloodshed in Afghanistan and Iraq united different groups in a common cause against America. US war planners had underestimated the difficulties of building a government from scratch following the defeat of Saddam Hussein in Iraq, and the country sank into chaos, leading to over 200,000 civilian killings between 2004 and 2007 and unimaginable suffering for innocent people. The scale of the war makes it difficult to determine the number of deaths, which were caused by famine and preventable diseases as well as direct violence, torture and murders, though the Costs of War Project at Brown University in 2023 indicated that the number is over 4.5 million.

The US census of the year 2000 counted 1.2 million people with Arab ancestry, like Naomi Shihab Nye. Following 9/11, these people found themselves living in a country waging war on their homelands. Many innocent Muslims, Arab Americans, Southeast Asians and other people perceived to be Middle Eastern became victims of hate crimes and discrimination. The consequences of the War on Terror changed the world forever.

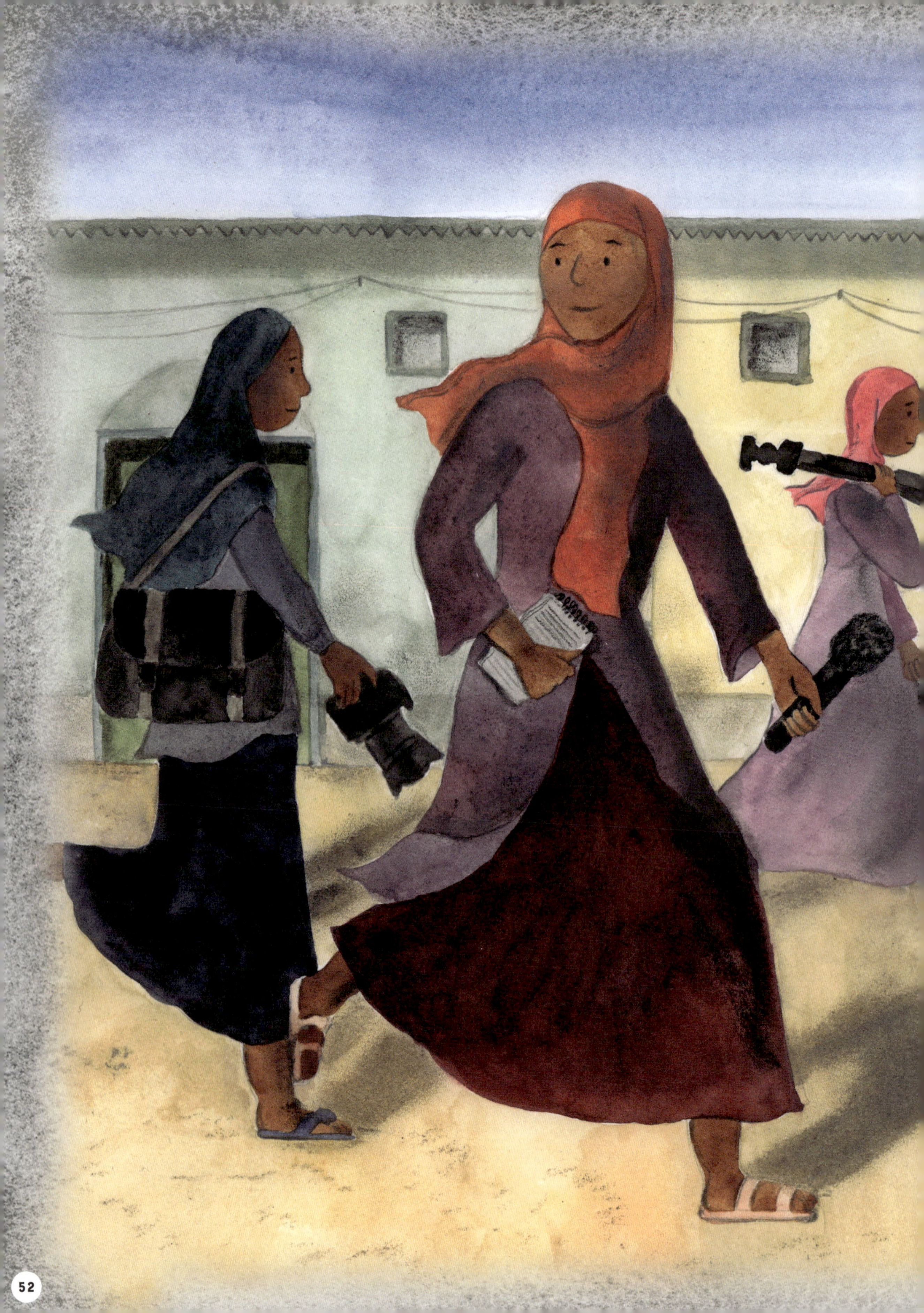

THE WRITER'S RIGHTS

ASHA LUL MOHAMUD YUSUF

Beginning extract

Journalists were discarded;
rights thrown in unmarked graves.
Men massacred; erased.
The press stripped of freedom.
Where is it officially written?
Where's the act or legislation?

Journalists were jailed,
crammed in cells with criminals,
or brought down in bullets,
their humanity denied.
There was no respect.
Where is it officially written?
Where's the act or legislation?

Injustice is infections,
your children are not safe,
your elders are not safe,
they will wipe out your women.
Mogadishu is worst.
If journalists wrote of wrongs,
why were they slaughtered?
My kinsmen, why the arrests?

The warlord's rope's a trap to trip
the public – to obstruct,
opposing peace, and hey you, thief!
Raiding our riches,
opening fire on our people.
You'll be called to account!

2008
Translated from Somali by Said Jama Hussein
and Muxamed Xasan 'Alto' with the poet Clare Pollard.

ASHA LUL MOHAMUD YUSUF

1977-

Asha Lul Mohamud Yusuf is a Somali poet.

Somali culture celebrates poetry, and so when Asha was young, she started to write her own poems. Her work began to get published on Somali websites in 2008, and since then she's received a lot of praise for her writing. Her collection *The Sea Migrations* was named the Poetry Book of the Year in 2018 by *The Sunday Times*. Asha's work concerns a lot of themes, including living in harmony with nature, paying tribute to lost lives, imploring Somalis to put aside their differences and heal, and the struggles of forced displacement and refugee life.

Asha came to the UK as a teenager in 1990 having fled the Somali Civil War. But through recordings, TV and the internet, her poems are reaching Somali people both at home and abroad.

THE SOMALI CIVIL WAR

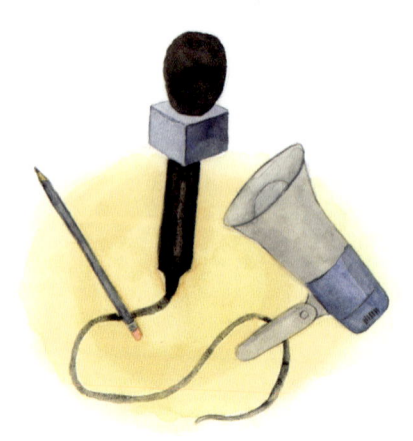

The Somali Civil War is an ongoing conflict. It was building for a long time, but sparked in 1991 when opposition groups overthrew the military government led by controversial leader Mohamed Siad Barre due to his increasingly oppressive and violent regime. This resulted in the collapse of Somalia's central government and the country being split into several regions, each controlled by a clan or a group of clans.

In May 1991, the region that was once British Somaliland declared independence as the Republic of Somaliland. Civil war broke out as clans fought for the territory. In 1998, the north-eastern part of Somalia, known as Puntland, also set up its own government. During the 1990s, more than 10 peace conferences were held to address the warfare in Somalia, but they were unsuccessful, and sadly all attempts at bringing together the warring groups failed. Much of Somalia, especially its capital Mogadishu, was a dangerous place to live during this period.

In addition to the violence in their country, Somali civilians suffered from frequent famines and starvation. A critical blow for the Somali people occurred in 2004 when a tsunami struck the coast, killing several hundred people, displacing many thousands more and destroying the livelihood of Somalia's fishing communities. Such starvation and suffering may lead people to turn to violence through desperation.

It has been very dangerous to be a journalist or a writer in Somalia. In 'The Writer's Rights', Asha writes of the right to freedom of expression and media freedom being restricted in her country. Some governments impose these restrictions to keep their citizens from learning about what's going on in their country and other parts of the world, to control them and to make rebellions less likely. Around the world, media restrictions lead to journalists being subjected to attacks from security forces, as well as threats, harassment, intimidation, arrests and even imprisonment. This prevents journalists from being able to report on what's happening – it strips away writers' rights. Though Yusuf's poem was written in 2008, Somalia's restrictions are still in place.

Over the last thirty years, tens of millions of Somali people who had to flee their homes have been displaced and separated from each other, initially in refugee camps and later settling in various countries around the world. The future of the Somali Civil War is uncertain, but the strength and resilience of the Somali people, such as Asha, continues to inspire.

LAMENT FOR SYRIA

AMINEH ABOU KERECH

Syrian doves croon above my head
their call cries in my eyes.
I'm trying to design a country
that will go with my poetry
and not get in the way when I'm thinking,
where soldiers don't walk over my face.
I'm trying to design a country
which will be worthy of me if I'm ever a poet
and make allowances if I burst into tears.
I'm trying to design a City
of Love, Peace, Concord and Virtue,
free of mess, war, wreckage and misery.

Oh Syria, my love
I hear your moaning
in the cries of the doves.
I hear your screaming cry.
I left your land and merciful soil
And your fragrance of jasmine
My wing is broken like your wing.

Syrian doves croon above my head
their call cries in my eyes.
I'm trying to design a country
that will go with my poetry
and not get in the way when I'm thinking,
where soldiers don't walk over my face.

I'm trying to design a country
which will be worthy of me if I'm ever a poet
and make allowances if I burst into tears.
I'm trying to design a City
of Love, Peace, Concord and Virtue,
free of mess, war, wreckage and misery.

Oh Syria, my love
I hear your moaning
in the cries of the doves.
I hear your screaming cry.
I left your land and merciful soil
And your fragrance of jasmine
My wing is broken like your wing.

I am from Syria
From a land where people pick up a discarded piece of bread
So that it does not get trampled on
From a place where a mother teaches her son not to step on an ant at the end of the day.
From a place where a teenager hides his cigarette from his old brother out of respect.
From a place where old ladies would water jasmine trees at dawn.
From the neighbours' coffee in the morning
From: after you, aunt; as you wish, uncle; with pleasure, sister . . .
From a place which endured, which waited, which is still waiting for relief.

Syria.
I will not write poetry for anyone else.

Can anyone teach me
how to make a homeland?
Heartfelt thanks if you can,
heartiest thanks,
from the house-sparrows,
the apple-trees of Syria,
and yours very sincerely.

2017

61

AMINEH ABOU KERECH

2004–

Amineh Abou Kerech is a Syrian writer.

When the Syrian Civil War broke out in 2011, Amineh was seven years old. She and her family moved around Syria for about two years, sleeping wherever they could find shelter, until they moved to Egypt.

After four and a half years in Egypt, Amineh and her family moved to Oxford, UK in the summer of 2016. A year after learning to speak English, she wrote 'Lament for Syria' when she was 13 years old. In 2017, 'Lament for Syria' won the Betjemen Prize, which is a poetry writing competition in the UK for young poets aged 10–13.

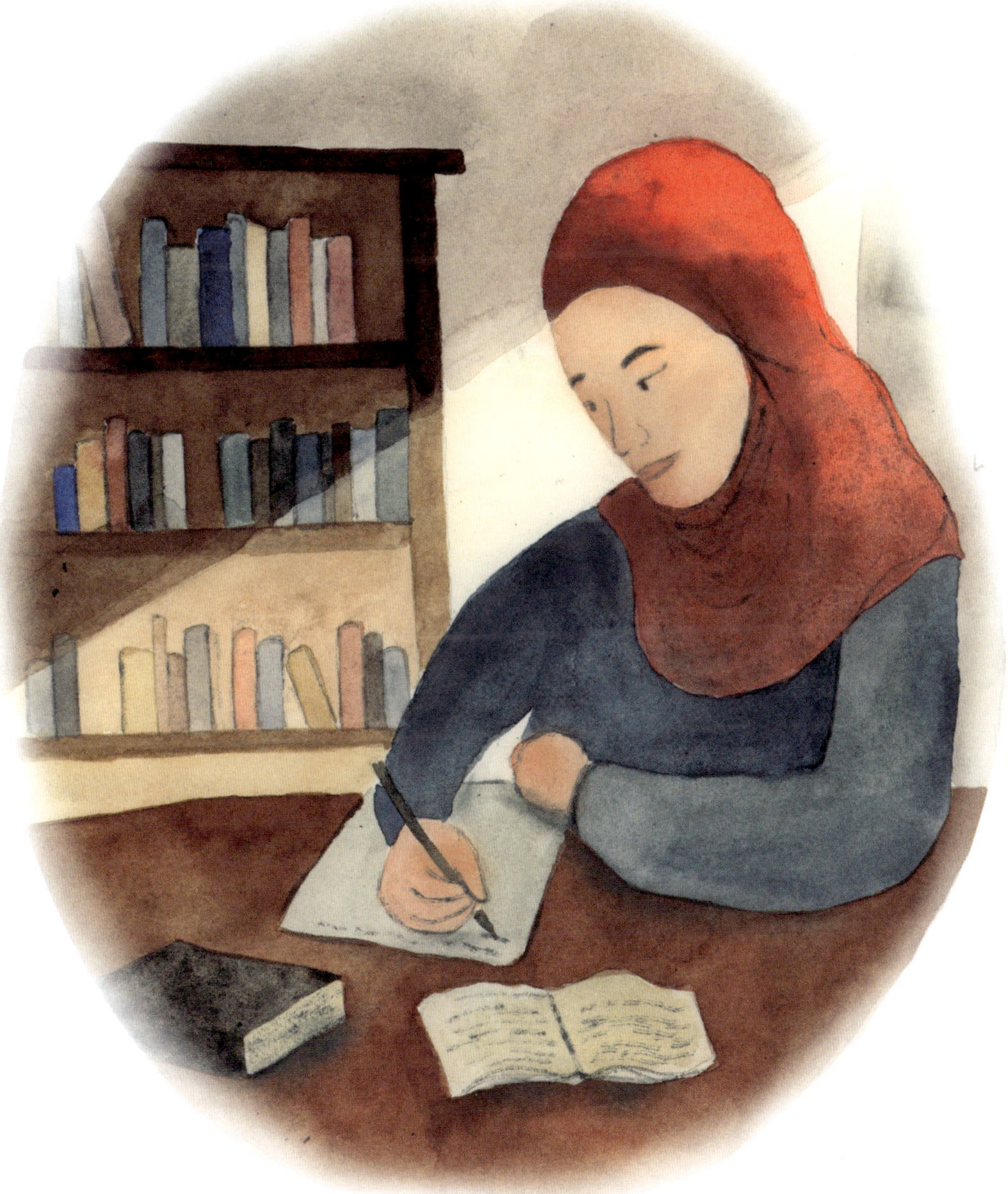

THE SYRIAN WAR

The Syrian War began as a revolution on 15 March 2011 as part of the Arab Spring, a wave of pro-democracy protests and uprisings that took place across the Middle East and North Africa in the early 2010s.

From 2006–2010, Syria suffered a terrible drought, which caused crops to fail and water shortages. The Syrian people were also unhappy about the high levels of unemployment and lack of political freedom, and many came to oppose the government of Syria and its leader, President Bashar al-Assad, whose family had ruled over Syria as a dictatorship for over 50 years. With this opposition, peaceful protests started in March 2011. However, the peaceful demonstrations were met by swift and deadly force used by the army and police, causing protests to break out across the country. The violence rapidly escalated, eventually giving way to a brutal war.

Many groups went on to join the war, with many fighting against each other. These groups include the Free Syrian Army (FSA), Kurdish Rebel Fighters, so-called Islamic State, Jabhat Fatah al-Sham, Hezbollah and the Syrian Democratic Forces (SDF). International involvement shaped the course of the conflict, too. Russia and Iran have backed the Syrian government, whereas the SDF were supported by the United States.

The word 'lament' used in the poem's title means a passionate expression of grief or sorrow. Many Syrians grieve for their home and the lives they've left behind, as the war has caused immense destruction in Syria and created the largest refugee population in the world. At least 11 million people have fled their homes in search of safety, just like Amineh Abou Kerech, which means more than half the country has lost their homes.

Syria is now free of the dictatorship as of December 2024, and hope can be seen within the country despite the extent of the destruction and divide caused by the conflict. Families continue to carry on their lives by creating homes, running schools and businesses, and giving children a sense of normality in displacement camps. Beyond Syria's borders, an emerging generation of young refugees are building their skills and seeking solutions, determined to rebuild their country when they can return. It is a new era for Syrians, one full of possibilities.

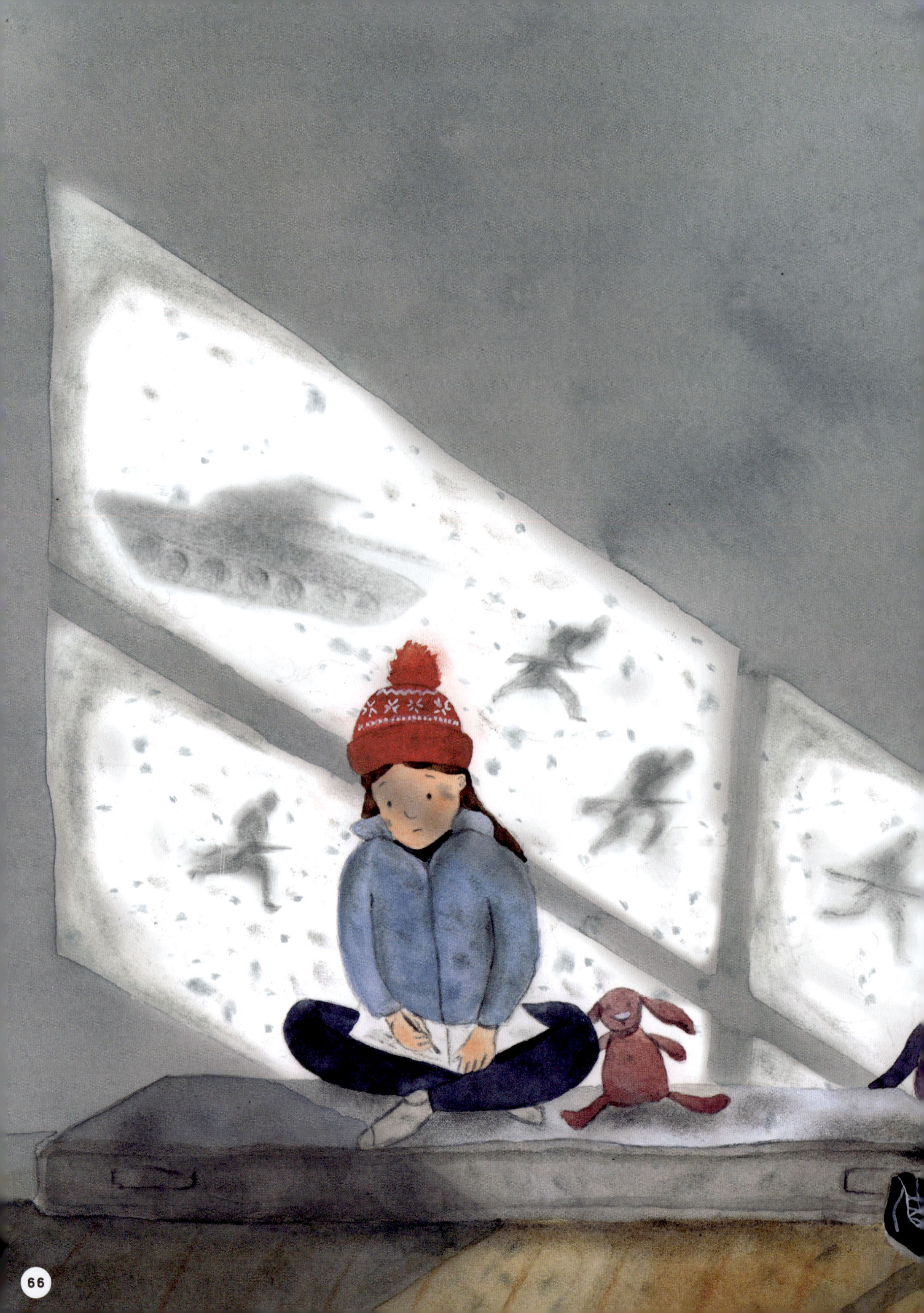

LETTERS TO A DEAD SOLDIER

MARIA DOCHEVA

Hi, Dad! How are you? We miss you.
Why don't you write to us? Do you have new friends?
You're on the front line, but what do you do?
Will you protect our region until this war ends?

Hi, Dad! Remember me? I'm Katy.
I'm by myself, writing to you again.
There were explosions. It was scary.
Mum is sleeping so I'm using her pen.

Hi, Daddy! If you sent us any letters,
we didn't read them, 'cause the post office was bombed.
There were victims . . . I hope things will get better.
I'm waiting for your letter – and you – back home!

Hi Dad, I'm writing alone again in fear,
because this morning my mummy . . .
The paper I'm writing on is covered in tears.
I'm not writing this letter to be funny.

Daddy, I'm sleeping in our neighbour's house tonight.
The old lady who was sometimes so rude
gave me drinks and clothes and a place to hide,
and she fed me some very tasty food.

Hey, Dad! Today is my birthday.
It's very important – I'm already seven!
I haven't received a letter from you today.
I hope this letter doesn't reach you in heaven.

Hey, Dad. I heard the neighbour saying
that you will not come back.
But why? Are your friends staying
to protect us from attacks?

But there were no more letters from her father
because on the bloody battlefield
the same soldier died slowly with the others.
Very soon his death will be revealed.

2023

Translated from Ukrainian by Maria Docheva

MARIA DOCHEVA

2011-

Maria Docheva is a Ukrainian student and writer, born in the seaside resort city of Odesa.

Maria has been an inquisitive and creative girl since her early childhood. In 2017, Maria started school with an in-depth study of English and mathematics, and she enjoys taking part in Olympiads both in mathematics and in English and Ukrainian. She loves reading books by various authors (both classical and modern) and writing poetry and prose, and she is also fond of singing.

Maria left Ukraine with her mother at the end of March 2022, and returned home over a year later in May 2023. She wrote 'Letters to a Dead Soldier', her collective image of all Ukrainian families affected by the war, when she was 12 years old.

THE RUSSIA-UKRAINE WAR

The Russia-Ukraine war is an ongoing conflict between Russia and Ukraine. The war began on 20 February 2014 and was a long time coming. The nation of Ukraine has been controlled by many different groups for hundreds of years. From 1922–1991, it was ruled by the Soviet Union, and before then it had been ruled by the Russian Empire. Ukraine became an independent country in 1991, but some still believed that the area should still be part of Russia, including the Russian president, Vladimir Putin.

In 2014, Putin sent troops to a region of Ukraine called Crimea. They took control of that region, and Putin supported people in the eastern section of Ukraine that wanted to join Russia.

By late 2021, Putin began building up troops along the Russian border with Ukraine, and on 24 February 2022, Putin invaded Ukraine with a ground and air strike campaign, in what has been described as the biggest attack on a European country since the Second World War. Ukrainian troops and civilians fought back, but many thousands fled to Poland, Romania and other countries to escape the fighting.

World leaders have condemned Putin for his actions and tried to stop the war by sending weapons to help Ukraine forces, as well as imposing sanctions (a punishment for disobeying rules and laws) on Russia for invading.

The war has taken a devastating toll on civilians. An estimated 5 million Ukrainian children, like Maria Docheva, were forced to flee their homes, and many had to escape alone after their family members went missing or were killed. It's not surprising that, sadly, lots of Ukrainian children are struggling with their mental health as the war continues. The conflict has also caused damage to vital infrastructure like internet and mobile phone networks, water pipes and electricity cables. Hundreds of schools have been damaged or destroyed.

Ukraine's President Zelensky says 'no one knows' when the war will end, and for now, the fighting continues.

WHERE DOES OUR POWER LIE?

JOSEPH COELHO

A poem about the feeling of powerlessness in modern times

Where does our power lie?
Another child screams ragged,
bloodied on our screens.
Another horror-of-civilians
caught in the crossfire - reels.

It feels infernal,
like there's 'MoreWarThanBefore',
a time of relative peace
but more aware than ever before,
more able to film the dying,
to report on every drop shed.

We toss fuseless petitions,
at feckless politicians.
growl at easy targets
to join us in toothless gesturing.
Browbeat all that don't march
to the rhythm of a skinless drum.
As we sever ourselves from the
screaming-silent
denied access to the world-wide-web.

Where does our power lie?
We fight a useless war
of one-upmanship,

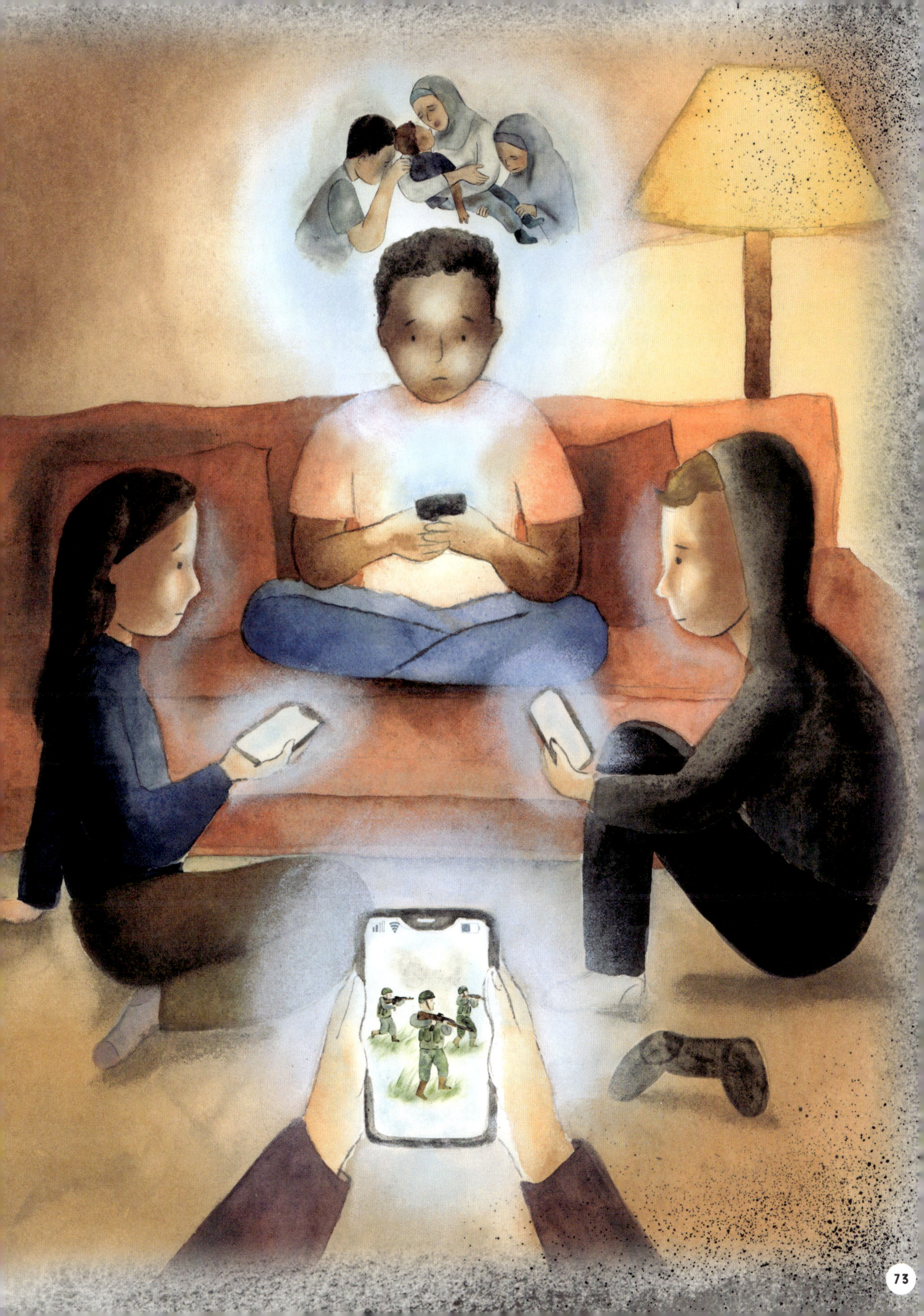

of discussion without end,
of painted morals and costume virtue.
as we parade the knowledge of our
complicity.

What might be possible
if we put down our posturing?
Remove the blinkers from our eyes?
Would we rid the powers of our
pounds?
Place ourselves in positions of power?
Help a neighbour?
Support a friend?
Do more than write a poem?

By Joseph Coelho

2024

JOSEPH COELHO O.B.E.
1980–

Joseph Coelho OBE, FRSL is a multi-award-winning children's author and playwright. His YA *The Girl Who Became a Tree: A story Told in Poems* was shortlisted for The 2021 Carnegie Medal and received a special mention from the Bologna Ragazzi Award 2021. He has written plays for Little Angel Theatre, Tutti Frutti Productions, Polka Theatre and The Unicorn Theatre amongst others. He is two-time winner of the Indie Book Awards (2019 & 2022) with picture books *If All The World Were* . . . and *My Beautiful Voice* respectively (illustrated by Allison Colpoys). His poetry collection *Werewolf Club Rules* (illustrated by John O'Leary) won the 2015 CLIPPA Poetry Award. His plays for adults have received a special commendation from the Verity Bargate Award and been longlisted for the Bruntwood Playwriting Competition. He won the 2024 Carnegie Medal for writing with *The Boy Lost In The Maze* (illustrated by Kate Milner) and was Waterstones Children's Laureate 2022–2024.

Coelho is committed to making the reading and writing of poetry accessible to everyone.

GLOSSARY

armistice – Peace agreement.

census – A count of all people and households in a country. People are asked questions about themselves, the people they live with, and their home. Census data is usually used for planning; for example, population and housing data might determine where schools are built.

civilian – A person not in the police or armed forces.

compulsory – Required by law or a rule.

conscription – Compulsory enlistment for state service, usually into the armed forces.

democracy – A country in which all citizens get to vote for their political leaders and representatives.

dictator – A ruler with total power over a country, often one who has taken control by force.

discrimination – When a person is treated unfairly because of who they are or characteristics that they have, such as their religion or their race.

displaced person – Someone who has been forced to flee from their home or homeland.

drought – A long period of unusually low rainfall, leading to a shortage of water.

economy – The way people spend money and make money.

empire – A group of territories ruled by one single ruler or state. Empires are built by countries that wish to control lands outside of their borders.

enrolment – Officially registering as a member of an institution like the armed forces.

genocide – Deliberately killing a large group of people because they are a certain nationality, race or religion.

hate crime – A crime, usually involving violence, that is motivated by hatred of someone's skin colour, religion, sexual orientation or other characteristic.

journalist – A person who gathers information by text, audio and pictures, turns it into news content and shares it with the public.

legislation – The process of making laws and putting them into practice.

nationalism – Loyalty and devotion to a nation.

persecution – Cruel and unfair treatment of a person or group, especially because of their religious or political beliefs, or their race.

propaganda – The spreading of biased or misleading information to promote a political cause.

racism – When people are treated unfairly because of their skin colour or background. It causes great harm to people and is a form of discrimination.

recruitment – The process of actively seeking out, finding and hiring people for a specific position or job.

refugee – A person who has been forced to leave their country to escape war and persecution.

secession – The act of withdrawing formally from the membership of something, especially splitting off from a country.

siege – A military operation in which enemy forces surround a town or building, cutting off essential supplies like food, with the aim of making those trapped inside surrender.

Soviet Union – A country that no longer exists, which was made up of fifteen republics in Eastern Europe and northern Asia.

territory – An area of land, sea or space connected with a particular country, person or animal.

terrorism – The use of violence and intimidation, especially against civilians, to try and achieve political aims. Counterterrorism is political or military activities designed to prevent or thwart terrorism.

unemployment – When people are not in a paid job and are available for work. Unemployment is often caused by a lack of jobs being available.

war correspondent – A journalist who covers stories first hand from a war zone.

CREDITS

'After a Bad Dream' by Gerrit Engelke,
English translation © Timothy Adès 2018

'The Butterfly' by Pavel Friedmann; from I NEVER SAW ANOTHER BUTTERFLY: CHILDREN'S DRAWINGS & POEMS FROM TEREZIN CONCENTRATION CAMP, 1942-44 edited by Hana Volavkova, copyright © 1978, 1993 by Artia, Prague. Compilation © 1993 by Penguin Random House LLC. Used by permission of Schocken Books, an imprint of the Knopf Doubleday Publishing Group, a division of Penguin Random House LLC. All rights reserved.

'The War' Text © 2020 Michael Rosen
From ON THE MOVE: POEMS ABOUT MIGRATION
Written by Michael Rosen & Illustrated by Quentin Blake.
Reproduced by permission of Walker Books Ltd,
London, SE11 5HJ www.walker.co.uk

Naomi Shihab Nye, 'During a War' from YOU & YOURS. Copyright © 2005 by Naomi Shihab Nye. Reprinted with the permission of The Permissions Company, LLC on behalf of BOA Editions, Ltd., boaeditions.org.

Extract from 'The Writer's Rights' by Asha Lul Mohamud Yusuf, translated from Somali by Said Jama Hussein and Maxamed Xasan 'Alto' with the poet Clare Pollard. First published in THE SEA-MIGRATIONS (Poetry Translation Centre / Bloodaxe Books, 2017). Reprinted with permission.

'The Writer's Rights'
Copyright © Asha Lul Mohamud Yusuf, Said Jama Hussein, Maxamed Xasan 'Alto', Clare Pollard 2017

'Lament for Syria'
Copyright © Amineh Abou Kerech 2017

'Letters to a Dead Soldier'
Copyright © Maria Docheva 2023
'Letters to a Dead Soldier'
English translation copyright © Maria Docheva 2025

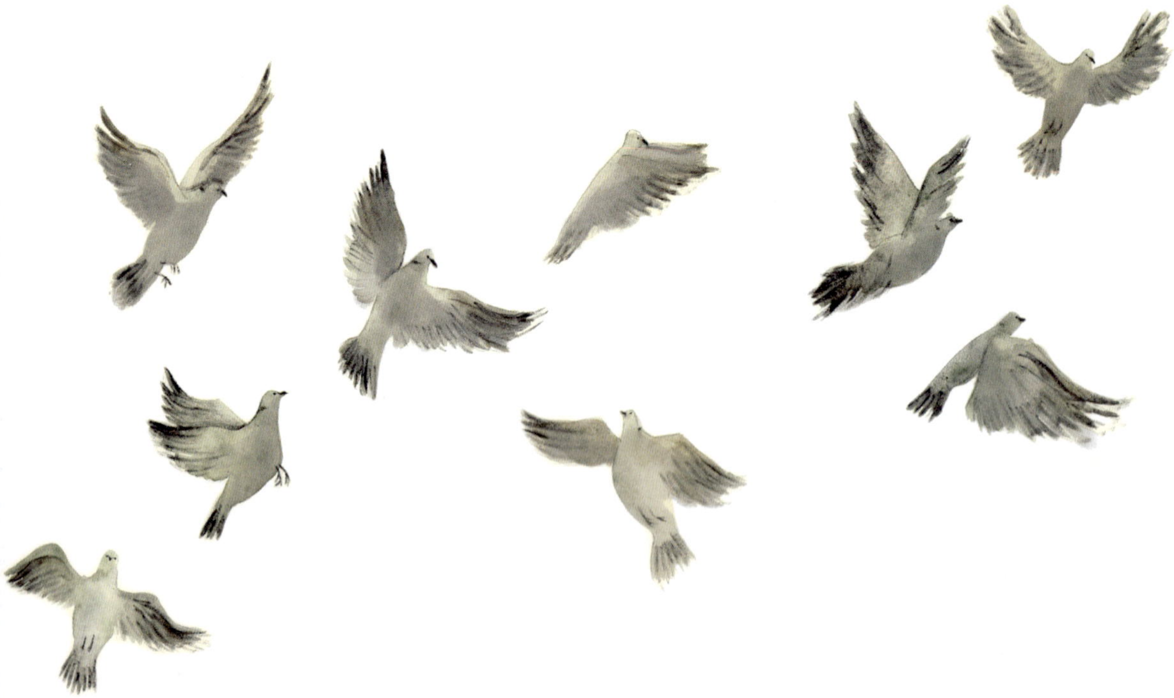

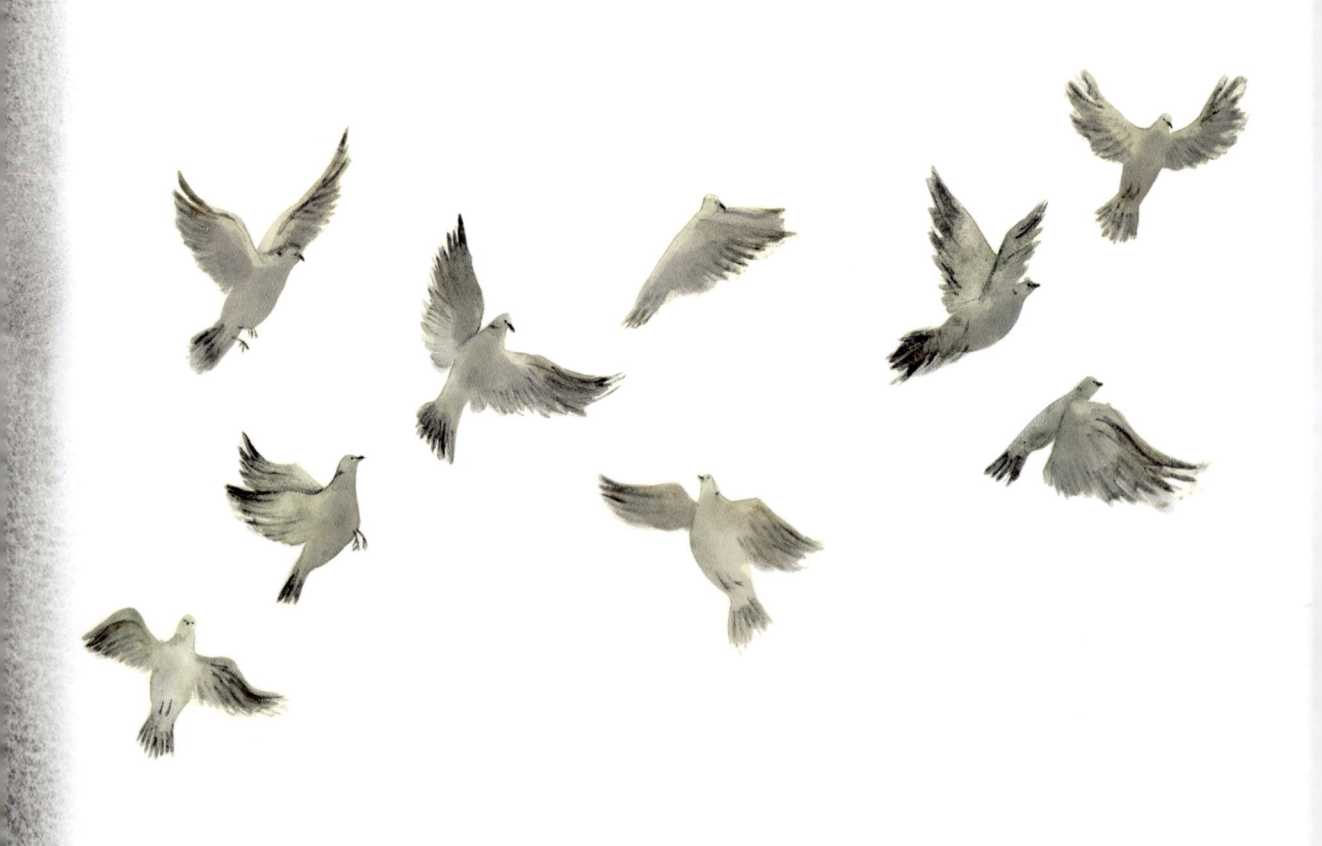